MW00424267

THE TITHE IS HOLY

Glen Johnson

Scripture quotations taken from the New King James Version. Copyright © 1982 by Thomas Nelson, Inc. Used by permission. All rights reserved.

Scripture quotations taken from the Amplified® Bible, Copyright © 1954, 1958, 1962, 1964, 1965, 1987 by The Lockman Foundation. Used by permission." (www.Lockman.org)

The Tithe Is Holy
ISBN: 978-1-7354232-2-7
Copyright (c)2020, Glen Johnson

Printed in the United States of America. All rights reserved under International Copyright Law. Contents and/or cover may not be reproduced in whole or in part in any form without the express written consent of the Publisher or Author.

ACKNOWLEDGMENTS

To my wife Theresa, I wouldn't be the man I am in my personal life or in ministry without you by my side for the past 32years of marriage. Faith Center wouldn't exist if not for your love, patience, and encouragement throughout the years.

To some of my friends and staff who helped see this project through to fruition, Taryn Trenda, Heather White, Katelyn Woltersdorf, Ashley Cathey, Scott Gorman, and Lisa Woltersdorf, thank you for always making me look better than I really am.

TABLE OF CONTENTS

CHAPTER ONE
WHY AREN'T WE BEING
BLESSED FINANCIALLY?

As I write this book, America is going through a time of economic trouble. Our country has been experiencing the worst recession since the 1920's. Businesses are closing, thousands of homes are in foreclosure, and bankruptcies are commonplace. Unemployment is off the charts and churches are struggling across the nation because the recession is affecting their offerings.

Even in my own church, many families have taken a financial hit. People have lost jobs and houses and felt the crunch in countless areas.

Where Is The God of Abundance?

As a pastor, it is my job to be a shepherd over the flock. A shepherd is to lead his flock into green pastures and beside still waters (Psalm 23:2).

So, after the first year of this recession, I started seeking the Lord about it. When I say I 'sought the Lord' I don't mean I was on my knees crying out to God. I simply started talking to Him, asking Him, "What's up, Lord? People in my congregation are givers and yet many of them are hurting financially during this recession! Why is that? Where is the God of abundance?"

The Bible says we're to get our financial wisdom from God, and He has promised to provide for us. One of the scriptures that shows us this is:

> Genesis 26:1-6 NKJV
> There was a famine in the land, besides the first famine that was in the days of Abraham. And Isaac went to Abimelech king of the Philistines, in Gerar. Then the Lord appeared to him and said: "Do not go down to Egypt; live in the land of which I shall tell you. Dwell in this land, and I will be with you and bless you; for to you and your descendants I give all these lands, and I will perform the oath which I swore to Abraham your father. And I will make your descendants multiply as the stars of heaven; I will give to your descendants all these lands; and in your seed all the nations of the earth shall be blessed; because Abraham obeyed My voice and kept My charge, My commandments, My statutes, and My laws." So Isaac dwelt in Gerar.

Here we see that Isaac had a covenant with God, yet there was a famine in his country, and he was lacking. He was considering a move to Egypt to get his financial increase and wisdom from there. God told Isaac to stay right where he was because that is where He had planted him. In verse 12 we see what happened when Isaac obeyed God:

> Genesis 26:12-13 NKJV
> Then Isaac sowed in that land, and reaped in the same year a hundredfold; and the Lord blessed him. The man began to prosper and continued prospering until he became very prosperous; for he had possessions of flocks and possessions of

herds and a great number of servants. So, the Philistines envied him.

From this we conclude that when people listen to God's wisdom, He can greatly prosper them, even in the midst of famine and financial trouble.

Increase When None Was Visible

The Bible is full of scriptural evidence of God's provision, right in the midst of lack.

> Psalms 9:9 AMP
> The Lord also will be a refuge and a high tower for the oppressed, a refuge and a stronghold in times of trouble (high cost, destitution, and desperation).

We see this in the New Testament too. In Luke 5:1-8, Peter had been out fishing all night long. When he came back in the morning, Jesus asked if He could use Peter's boat. After He preached from the boat, Jesus told Peter to throw the fishing nets out on the other side for a catch.

Now, Peter was trying to be nice because Jesus was a Man of God, but he basically said, "Reverend, You don't have any idea what You're talking about. I fished all night and didn't catch anything, and now it's daylight, when no one catches fish! Nevertheless, because You said to, I will let down my net."

And in a time when fish were not supposed to be there (when there was not supposed to be any financial increase happening) Peter let down his net, in obedience to God's wisdom, and caught so many fish that the net started breaking!

But let's look at verses 4 & 5, again.

> Luke 5:4-5 NKJV
> When He had stopped speaking, He said to Simon, "Launch out into the deep and let down your nets for a catch." But Simon answered and said to Him, "Master, we have toiled all night and caught nothing; never-the-less at Your word I will let down the net." And when they had done this, they caught a great number of fish, and their net was breaking.

Notice Jesus told Peter to let down nets (plural) and Peter let down the net (singular). Peter actually missed out on a bigger blessing that Jesus had for him because he was so focused on the fact he had already been fishing and had caught nothing. He was physically doing it, but on the in-side he was telling Jesus, "Hey I'm the fisherman here and we just got back in from fishing all night and didn't catch anything. But because you are Jesus I'll obediently go throw a net out." If he would only have listened, really listened, to what Jesus had said, his blessing may have been substantially larger.

How many times do we do this? We say to ourselves, "I've tried that already and it didn't work!" Our attitude often holds us back from the blessing Jesus has for us.

So Where's Our Blessing?

Again in Matthew 17:24-27, God provides when Jesus and the disciples needed to pay taxes. At a time when they didn't have it in their pockets, Jesus told Peter to go down to the lake and get the tax money from a fish's mouth. And he did!

In John 6:5-13, Jesus was preaching to 5,000 people who had been out in the wilderness with Him so long, they were hungry. They weren't anywhere near food and they didn't have any provisions along to feed all those people. We see God's abundance flow again. Jesus blessed a little boy's lunch of loaves and fishes, and they all got fed with 12 baskets of food left over!

As I read the Word, I saw God again and again bringing people abundance in time of famine. The Bible is giving us stories and examples to help us in our current situations. If this principle doesn't work today, then it's not any good. But it does work!

So, the cry of my heart for my flock and for our church, was, "Where is this abundance, Lord? We've cut back, budgeted well, and tried to be people of integrity (thinking that somehow because we are people of integrity we'll be blessed), yet we keep going backwards! Where's our blessing that You have promised in your Word?"

A Word from God

I've been a Christian since 1978. Since that time, I have heard the Lord's voice five times in this manner. The first time was when I got born again. At the time, I was putting off this person who was witnessing to me, and I heard the Lord's voice inside of me. I can't really describe it other than to say it was this very strong impression or voice; I call it the voice of many waters as Revelation does (Rev. 1:15; 14:2). It was this voice of many waters that said to me, "IT'S NOW OR NEVER!" So, I thought, "I think I will get saved right now." And I did!

The second time God has spoken to me in this manner was about how to be refreshed in prayer as Jesus was. Whenever Jesus did miracles He went alone to pray. The third time He talked to me about praying for an Arab leader who has now passed away. The fourth time He talked to me about changing the way our church did communion. All of this occurred over the span of 30 years.

The fifth time was on January 26, 2010 (or 2011?) at 1:15am, I suddenly woke up from a deep sleep and God spoke four words very loud and clear in my heart, "THE TITHE IS HOLY!"

When He spoke the words, immediately revelation began to come. Scriptures began to open up to me. Things I thought I understood before began making even more sense and were revealed to me.

We, as parents, want our children blessed abundantly. We know God is a God of abundance and He wants to see His children blessed as well. Religion makes us feel that God is out to get us. In this assumption, the world doesn't always look at God as a loving father, but as if He is just sitting up in Heaven waiting for us to make one wrong move, and then He will zap us.

That doesn't sound like a God of abundance or of blessings! Let's put our faith into action and begin believing that God has more for us. Maybe it's time to try something bigger, act bigger, and believe for abundant blessings. He has more than enough to provide for us as His children. We just have to renew our mind to how big He is and not settle for less! God wants to bless us!!

Testimony

Jim and LuAnn

We had been going to FCC for over 10 years but had never really tithed. We believed in tithing and heard all the incredible testimonies about what tithing had done for people but when it came to payday we always had other uses for our money.

Jim got laid off from his job in August 2010 and my overtime at work was cut out. Within a two-week period of time, our income was cut in half! The problem was that our bills weren't cut in half and didn't have control over our spending. Due to not budgeting correctly when we did have 2 incomes, we were behind on our bills. Each month we seemed to get farther and farther behind.

In December it really all came to a head. We couldn't pay all our rent. Our landlord was willing to work with us, which was great, but he couldn't do it forever. In January we couldn't pay all our rent either. He said that he had to have all the rent for February, or he would have to give us a 20-day notice. He could not continue to carry us.

On February 5, Pastor Glen started his message The Tithe is Holy. We had heard this type of teaching before but it never really hit home. But this time we were desperate. During the tithe and offering period that Sunday God kept telling me to give what we had and He would provide the rest. I just couldn't do it. My faith was not at that level. I had no problem with faith for healing but finances were a different story. Finally, toward the end of service I gave in. We took the last $10 that we had and put it in the envelope and prayed. "God, this is all we have and out of obedience we are giving it to You. You know the financial situation that we are in and only You can fix it." We knew that God was faithful even when we weren't.

On February 8th we were given a 20-day notice by our landlord. He said we needed to come up with $600, which was the rest of February's rent, and he would void the notice and work with us on the back rent we owed. We stood firm knowing that God had to provide it. Someone from church gave us $250 that week which was a great help. On Thursday, a friend of mine from work said she knew we were having financial problems (I hadn't told her about the notice we received) and she handed me an envelope with $500 in it. She said we didn't have to pay her back until the end of the year! Praise God!

Just a few days after giving God the last of our money He paid the rent and we still had money for groceries! But He wasn't done. Thursday night another friend of ours called and said he and his wife had received some unexpected money and they wanted to give it to us to help us pay a bill or two! We were able to get two bills paid with that and God still wasn't done!

I also had a garnishment coming out of my paycheck which had been taking over $300 from each of my paychecks since December. On that same Thursday, I called my payroll processing center to find out what I had to do to lower the amount that was being taken from each check. The woman I spoke to said there no longer was a garnishment on my check!

My husband and I had a heart change on that Sunday, February 6, 2011. We have tithed on everything we have received since then and now my husband is back to work also!

CHAPTER TWO
THE TITHE IS HOLY

When the Lord spoke those four words to me, understanding began to flow into me like a computer download from heaven. I began to see clearly what He meant, and how we have made the tithe, in some ways, unholy.

> Leviticus 27:30 NKJV
> And all the tithe of the land, whether of the seed
> of the land or of the fruit of the tree, is the Lord's.
> It is holy to the Lord.

I began to understand that there are two ways we have made the tithe unholy: (1) by refusing to tithe because of doctrinal issues, budget, rebellion, or fear and (2) we don't worship God with our tithe; it just gets thrown into a bucket, with very little thought. Maybe, doctrinally speaking, we disagree with tithing. Maybe we have blown our budget so bad that if we tithed, we couldn't pay our house payment. Maybe we are in rebellion and decide that we aren't going to obey the Lord no matter what He wants us to do. Or, maybe we're afraid that if we tithe, we won't have enough money left for other things.

So, the number one way we keep the tithe unholy is by refusing to do it. The Bible said that the tithe is the Lord's, and it is holy to Him.

An Acceptable Sacrifice

Next, I saw that the way we tithe has been unholy. We've just been throwing it in the bucket or offering plate. We haven't been worshipping God with our tithe. I began to go back and study the Bible in earnest on tithes and offerings. One of those scriptures that flooded over me when God spoke to me was:

> Philippians 4:15-18 NKJV
> Now you Philippians know also that in the beginning of the gospel, when I departed from Macedonia, no church shared with me concerning giving and receiving but you only. For even in Thessalonica you sent aid once and again for my necessities. Not that I seek the gift, but I seek the fruit that abounds to your account. Indeed, I have all and abound. I am full, having received from Epaphroditus the things sent from you, a sweet-smelling aroma, an acceptable sacrifice, well pleasing to God.

I have read that scripture dozens of times, yet something I had never seen before jumped out at me. Notice it says, "A sweet-smelling aroma, an acceptable sacrifice..." If there is an acceptable sacrifice, that must mean there is an unacceptable sacrifice as well. So, can we give an offering as an unacceptable sacrifice to the Lord?

In Genesis 4:1-7, we see the story of Cain and Abel. In verse 5, it says, God did not respect Cain or his offering. Cain's offering was unacceptable to God. Scripture isn't clear on why this was so, but it is very clear that Abel's offering was acceptable and Cain's was not. Keeping our tithe holy will assure us of making our offering's acceptable to God.

But when you give it as an acceptable sacrifice, Philippians 4:19, says, "And my God shall supply all your need according to His riches in glory by Christ Jesus."

Read that verse again -- He will meet our need according to His riches in glory by Christ Jesus. That does not mean He'll meet our need "according to the great world recession that is going on." No, it says "ac-cording to His riches in glory by Christ Jesus!" If it doesn't work in finances, then why would I believe it for salvation? But it does work!

We Changed the Process

I began to see how we had been giving the tithe in an unholy manner. After worship, the congregation would sit down, we'd do the announcements, then it was time to take the offering. I would talk about giving and receiving for a minute, then we'd pass the buckets.

Then the video announcements would come up, and during the time the tithe was being received, people would text on their phones, talk to their neighbor, or go to the bathroom. We were acting like the offering time was over after I talked about it. After that, it was just "the collection" part of the offering, which we did very casually.

But as I began to look in the Bible about tithing, I saw some things. I thought to myself, "What if we took communion the same way we've been receiving the offering?" If we took communion and people were talking to each other, texting on their phones, and going to the bathroom, you would say, "That's crazy! That's out of order! This is holy communion!" And notice: the Bible doesn't say anywhere that communion is holy. But it does say that the tithe is holy.

After I saw that, we changed the whole process in our church of how we took the offering. Sometimes we put the buckets up front. Not because it's somehow holier up on the platform than it is in the chairs, but because we want the giving of our tithes and offerings to be a time of worship to the Lord. We go right from our worship time of singing praises to God to talking about giving to God. As we collect the tithes and offerings, we continue worshipping and people bring them to the front worshipping the Lord as they come.

Families are joining together as a family unit, either in their chairs or in the front, as they pray and present their offering to the Lord. Single people are joining other single people and presenting their offering together. People are now standing at the alter praying over their precious seed they are presenting to the Lord. It is no longer a bill being thrown into the bucket and then talking to your neighbor about their upcoming week, or where they want to go to lunch, but it is now truly a part of worship to the Lord.

Testimony

Jay and Isabel

Pastor Glen came and taught "The Tithe is Holy" in our church. His message helped us tremendously both individually and as a church, sparking us to treat the offering of our tithes as a holy event in which we worship the Lord. This has changed our hearts and attitude towards Jesus as High Priest of the tithe and caused a twenty-five percent increase in our church body's monthly giving.

CHAPTER THREE
DO I HAVE TO TITHE?

The first known tithe is in Genesis 14. People say that tithing was under the law and it was, but it was before, during, and after the law. The tithe was a principle before the law and now that the law has been fulfilled, there is no law that says you have to tithe. Understand, tithing isn't a "have to" deal! If you believe in Jesus and die but don't tithe you will still go to heaven. You are not going to hell if you don't tithe. You just may not be as prosperous as some. God is trying to bless us. He is trying to tell us something. I believe I am speaking a prophetic word to you here that can sustain you in times of trouble! It can get you through a bad economy and prosper you on the other side!

The First Tithe

Let's go all the way back and look at that first tithe.

> Genesis 14:14-20 NKJV (With my additions)
> Now when Abram heard that his brother was taken captive, he armed his three hundred and eighteen trained servants who were born in his own house, and went in pursuit as far as Dan. He divided his forces against them by night, and he and his servants attacked them and pursued them as far as Hobah, which is north of Damascus. So, he brought back all the goods, and also brought back his brother Lot and his goods, as well as the women and the people. And the king of Sodom

went out to meet him at the Valley of Shaveh (that is, the King's Valley), after his return from the defeat of Chedorlaomer and the kings who were with him. Then Melchizedek king of Salem brought out bread and wine (sounds like a holy thing, doesn't it?); he was the priest of God Most High. And he blessed him and said: "Blessed be Abram of God Most High, Possessor of heaven and earth; And blessed be God Most High, Who has delivered your enemies into your hand." And he gave him a tithe of all.

Now watch this. Here the king of Sodom tries to talk Abram out of tithing. Verse 21 says: Now the king of Sodom said to Abram, "Give me the persons, and take the goods for yourself." In other words, the king said, "You don't need to tithe. Just give me something out of this and take the rest for yourself."

Genesis 14:22,23 NKJV
But Abram said to the king of Sodom, "I have raised my hand to the Lord, God Most High, the Possessor of heaven and earth, that I will take nothing, from a thread to a sandal strap, and that I will not take anything that is yours, lest you should say, 'I have made Abram rich.'

So, this is when Abram gave the first tithe. He didn't give it out of awe or obligation -- he gave it because he loved God and the tithe is about giving God honor for what He has done for you, and offerings are to say "God, this is what I believe that You are going to do for us in the future."

Tithing in the New Testament

Tithing isn't mentioned much in the New Testament, but worship is hardly mentioned in the New Testament either. Yet we don't disregard it. We get our instruction on worship from the Old Testament (and from what I can see, if you compare our worship services today with the aggressive worship in the Old Testament, we are at about 10%!). Our New Testament scripture for the tithe is Hebrews 7. I have studied Hebrews extensively, and it's a very interesting study when you get into chapter 7.

The subject of chapter 7 is not really tithing, but rather honoring God. Tithing was always a principle that was paid to somebody greater than yourself. Hebrews 7:9 talks about Levi paying tithes through Abraham in this way. When you and I are paying our tithe, it is to something greater than ourselves. We don't take our tithe and pay our kid's tuition with it, or use it for anything material. We are to honor God with our tithe.

> Hebrews 7:1-9 NKJV (With my additions)
> For this Melchizedek, king of Salem, priest of the Most High God, who met Abraham returning from the slaughter of the kings and blessed him, to whom also Abraham gave a tenth part of all, first being translated "king of righteousness," and then also king of Salem, meaning "king of peace," without father, without mother, without genealogy, having neither beginning of days nor end of life, but made like the Son of God, remains a priest continually. Now consider how great this man was, to whom even the patriarch Abraham gave a tenth of the spoils. And indeed those who are of the sons of Levi, who receive the priesthood, have a commandment to receive tithes from the people according to the law, that is, from their brethren, though they have come from the loins of Abraham; but he whose genealogy is not derived from them received

tithes from Abraham and blessed him who had the promises. Now beyond all contradiction the lesser is blessed by the better. Here (right now, today) mortal men receive tithes, but there he (Jesus) receives them, of whom it is witnessed that he lives. Even Levi, who receives tithes, paid tithes (through) Abraham.

Notice verse 8 says that men who die – mortal men – receive tithes. How does that work?

In church, we put our offering in the bucket and the ushers carry it out, then it goes into the safe, then on Monday it gets counted and that's how the church receives it. Then it's used to provide classes for children, youth church, reach out to our community, pay the utilities, provides staff and building maintenance, so that the church can provide a place of spiritual nourishment for you. That's how men who die receive the tithes.

In my church, we are good stewards. We are not frivolous. I have never paid a bill late in our churches history since 1982. We don't even take a stamp from the office to mail something personal. We buy that stamp from the office. There is integrity in all our dealings. I think that's very important. We receive the tithe and we want to be the best stewards we can possibly be of the tithe, because verse 8 goes on to say, "...there He receives them, of whom it is witnessed that He lives."

Jesus Receives the Tithe

Verse 3 compares Jesus to Melchizedek. Think about this: in all the Old Testament, the only thing we can find that Melchizedek did was to receive Abram's tithe. Some people think he was an Old Testament appearance of Jesus, but we don't know that. The only reason he existed, that we know of, was to receive the tithe from Abram.

I submit to you that if Melchizedek indeed was the appearance of Jesus, then the tithe is so holy that one of the jobs of Jesus, at the right hand of the Father, is to receive your tithe. That obviously makes the tithe very holy.

1 Corinthians 16:2 says, "On the first day of the week let each one of you lay something aside..." They took the first day of the week to honor God with their giving and we can also. The first day of the week was the day they choose to be a day of honoring the Lord with their giving. My assumption is they looked at that day as special, a holy day. So we see that the tithe is holy, and we tithe to honor God. Honoring the Lord with our tithe is a wonderful thing we get to do. Notice I didn't say we have to do, that would be law. We choose to honor God and present our tithe to Him. By doing this we are showing him we trust Him to take care of us. It is as if we placed our tithe on our open hand, stretching it out to God.

Honoring the Lord with our tithe is a wonderful thing we get to do. Notice I didn't say we "have to"; that would be law. We choose to honor God and present our tithe to Him.

By doing this. we are showing Him we trust Him to take care of us. It is as if we have placed our tithe on our open hand, stretching it out to God.

Testimony

Abe

I have been a tither my whole life. I received this teaching from Pastor Glen and decided to put it into practice in all areas of my life. At 17 I would work 6 hours but only claim 4 hours on my time card. I was believing God for extra money for school. I was given an unexpected check for $2,000.00

CHAPTER FOUR
AM I CURSED IF I DON'T TITHE?

As I continued to look into the Word, the book of Malachi (which most faith people and preachers totally misunderstand) began to open up to me. Many of us have heard or used Malachi chapter 3 to talk about the tithe.

> Malachi 3:7-12 NKJV
> Yet from the days of your fathers you have gone away from My ordinances and have not kept them. Return to Me, and I will return to you," says the Lord of hosts. "But you said, 'In what way shall we return?' Will a man rob God? Yet you have robbed Me! But you say, 'In what way have we robbed You?' In tithes and offerings. You are cursed with a curse, for you have robbed Me, even this whole nation. Bring all the tithes into the storehouse, that there may be food in My house, and try Me now in this," says the Lord of hosts, "if I will not open for you the windows of heaven and pour out for you such blessing that there will not be room enough to receive it. And I will rebuke the devourer for your sakes, so that he will not destroy the fruit of your ground, nor shall the vine fail to bear fruit for you in the field," says the Lord of hosts; and all nations will call you blessed, for you will be a delightful land," says the Lord of hosts.

It says: "Will a man rob God? Yet you have robbed Me! But you say, 'In what way have we robbed You?' In tithes and offerings. You are cursed with a curse..." There are many people, myself included, who have preached that if you don't tithe you are cursed. But wait – let's analyze and think more carefully about some of these things.

The Christian Curse?

Let's say you are not saved and do not know the Lord Jesus. You come to church with a friend, the Gospel gets preached to you, and you come up to the altar to get saved.

You hadn't been tithing before because you didn't care about God. Or maybe you only went to church on Christmas and Easter and tipped Him five bucks. You thought He would be mad if you didn't put something in the offering bucket.

But now you've gotten saved. Does that mean that the following Sunday, when you don't throw your tithe in the bucket, now you have a curse on you? You didn't have a curse on you before, but now you get "The Christian Curse" because you didn't tithe? If you think about it, that is really what some people have been preaching all these years; "The Christian Curse" is brought on by not tithing.

This makes so much more sense now that the whole revelation came to me! He is not saying you are cursed with a curse if you don't tithe. He is just pointing out what has already happened to your financial situation.

Using some paraphrasing, what God is really saying in Malachi is, "Would you try it My way? Look at what you are doing! You are cursed with a curse. Living the world's way is not working for you! Nothing that you are doing is working for you. It seems like your car is always breaking down. It seems like every time you turn around the vacuum cleaner breaks, or this breaks and that breaks. Just look at your life! You are cursed with a curse! Would you try it My way?" says the Lord.

God, I trust You

God is saying, "Return to me and I will return to you." How do we return to Him? Here's how to do it: take 10% (tithe means 10%) and give it to Him.

When we do that, we are bowing our knee, inwardly or outwardly, and saying, "Father, I trust You. You are my covenant keeper. When I tithe, I am trusting You with my whole financial situation. I humbly bring a heart of love for You, and I give this tithe as a holy offering to You. You are my God, take care of me. The Lord is my Shepherd I shall not want. Lord, I acknowledge You as my Shepherd today."

If we brought the tithe like that, I can't see the Lord saying, "Tough luck buddy!" No, I believe He would say "Wow! I am going to produce for that child of mine! I am going to work on their behalf!"

The Natural AND the Supernatural

It has to be mentioned that budgeting and stewardship are part of prospering, because you can get the best job in the world and be totally in debt, asking why God isn't meeting your needs. Anyone can be foolish with the money they have!

I've also seen the Lord provide the perfect job for someone – their dream job – but they were an absolute jerk to work with and they got fired. That's not God's fault! What I am saying is simply this, budgeting is great. All those things are important, and we need to learn, budget, work hard, and to do the best we can with what we have.

But in reality, where is the supernatural power of God? Where is the net-breaking, boat-sinking, catch? Where is the sowing-in-famine and receiving one-hundred-fold? I am telling you prophetically, the tithe is holy.

Take 10% of your income and honor the Lord with it. Don't just give it grudgingly. Tithe with an attitude that says, "God, I trust You and I honor You with my tithe." If you do, I believe you will see the same supernatural things in your life that God has shown us in His Word. Tithing brings us out of the financial curse of the world and into the financial blessing from heaven.

Money is such a touchy area in many people's lives. Many families never talk about finances. From one generation to the next, nothing is disclosed about our state of affairs because we hold our precious finances so close to our chest. We don't want others to know what we do or don't have, but God knows the state of our affairs.

God wants to help take you to the next level in your finances. He wants us to have an abundance for every good work as 2 Corinthians 9:8 says. "And God is able to bless you abundantly, so that in all things at all times, having all that you need, you will abound in every good work."

The world doesn't seem to get ahead, but God's system is a system of abundance. You begin to tithe and at first you think there is no way this will work. You barely have enough as it is. But you have decided to get your finances onto God's system, so you bite the bullet and go for it. You are at church and every devil in hell is suddenly reminding you of all the things you need to spend that tithe on. You get an envelope, your palms are sweating, your heart is racing, but you continue to fill it out. You now need to go to the offering buckets and present it to the Lord. Your knees begin wobbling as you walk to the front, pray, and drop the tithe in the bucket.

In the next few days, you continue to confess that all your needs are met, because He takes care of his children. Then Friday comes along and you have a financial blessing occur! Now you can really say in your heart that He supplies all your needs!

Testimony

Haley & Matt

We both were out of work, so our finances were dismal. As a result, we had quit giving. After listening to this teaching, we decided enough is enough and gave. The next day Matt was called to do some side work. The following Sunday, we went online and gave because we were out of town. That Monday Haley got called for a job interview. Afterwards she said, there were others much more qualified than her. She got called back Wednesday to interview with the president. Three people interviewed with the president and she left thinking, it looks pretty good! AND she got the job!!

CHAPTER FIVE
WHAT YOUR TITHE SAYS ABOUT YOU

The tithe declares our total dependence upon God. When you place your hard-earned dollars, your tithe, into the offering bucket you are saying "God, I trust you in the financial realm. I'm honoring You with my seed, my finances."

Earlier, in Malachi, we cleared up the whole issue about being under a curse if you don't tithe. That is not what the Lord was saying there. If you look at it in the context, He was saying, "Try it my way."

I am not trying to teach the tithe out of some religious obligation– the tithe isn't from the law. You aren't going to get closer to God or get to Heaven if you tithe, just as you aren't breaking some law if you don't tithe. I am trying to tell you how to get on board with God's financial system of doing things! I believe I am giving you something that will sustain and help you, through good times and bad.

Your Faith Pleases God

Hebrews 11:6 NKJV
But without faith it is impossible to please Him, for he who comes to God must believe that He is, and that He is a rewarder of those who diligently seek Him.

Is there any greater act of faith than getting paid, taking 10% of your hard-earned money, and putting it in the offering bucket? That takes faith! When you do that, what you're saying to God is, "God, this is my acknowledgment that I trust You. I set your Word in motion and I'm believing You are a rewarder." Without faith it is impossible to please Him. So, there has to be acts of faith to please God.

I am a literalist when it comes to the Bible, I believe that the Bible is literal. But when it talks about certain things – worshipping Him, loving your spouse, doing good – there is no scripture that specifically says those actions please Him. There are a lot of things in the Bible that probably please God, but this scripture in Hebrews 11:6 is the only one I know of that specifically says, "this pleases God -- faith."

Well, I want to be a God-pleaser. I'm sure you do too. Our faith pleases Him. Tithing is an act of faith. I believe that pleases God. I think that He just loves that part of it, where we just totally abandon ourselves and trust Him.

The Tithe Locates Our Heart

Matthew 6:21 says, "Where your treasure is, there will your heart be also." We can tell where someone's heart is by where they spend their money.

Abraham's Sacrifice

Genesis 22 is the story of Abraham, and his son Isaac. Abraham was old when God promised him that he was going to have a son. He and his wife had tried to have children for years and couldn't, yet they had this son in their old age because of the promise of God. Abraham was 100 years old when Isaac was born (Gen 21:5).

Then after this long-awaited child was born, while Isaac was still young, God told Abraham to take him up on the mountain and sacrifice him. Wow! That is some heavy stuff! The only begotten son! Let's pick the story up in verse 3.

> Genesis 22:3-5 NKJV
> So Abraham rose early in the morning and saddled his donkey, and took two of his young men with him, and Isaac his son; and he split the wood for the burnt offering, and arose and went to the place of which God had told him. Then on the third day Abraham lifted his eyes and saw the place afar off. And Abraham said to his young men, "Stay here with the donkey; the lad and I will go yonder and worship, and we will come back to you."

Abraham was going to do what he was told to do, but he was believing God that something supernatural was going to happen. He believed that if he killed his son, God was going to raise him from the dead.

> Genesis 22:6-12 NKJV
> So Abraham took the wood of the burnt offering and laid it on Isaac his son; and he took the fire in his hand, and a knife, and the two of them went together. But Isaac spoke to Abraham his father and said, "My father!" And he said, "Here I am, my son." Then he said, "Look, the fire and the wood, but where is the lamb for a burnt offering?" And Abraham said, "My son, God will provide for Himself the lamb for a burnt offering." So the two of them went together. Then they came to the place of which God had told him. And Abraham built an altar there and placed the wood in order;

> and he bound Isaac his son and laid him on the altar, upon the wood. And Abraham stretched out his hand and took the knife to slay his son. But the Angel of the Lord called to him from heaven and said, "Abraham, Abraham!" So he said, "Here I am." And He said, "Do not lay your hand on the lad, or do anything to him; for now I know that you fear God, since you have not withheld your son, your only son, from Me."

Notice that God said, "...for NOW I know...." We always say that God knows our heart. Did God know Abraham's heart? We would have said that He did. But here he says "...for now I know..." So, there must be acts of obedience or acts of faith that prove things to God, to let Him know we're ready to get to the next place in our life.

At the end of the story, God provided a ram for the sacrifice, and Abraham killed the ram instead of Isaac. Then Abraham called God Jehovah- Jireh (Gen. 22:14) which means "the Lord my Provider." But notice that Abraham had to be obedient and go ahead with an act of faith beforehand, and then discovered the Lord was his provider.

So, God said in verse 12, "...for now I know..." God didn't know Abraham's heart until there was an act of obedience. Apparently, God doesn't know our hearts the way we think He does -- whether we will or we won't do what He's said -- until there's an action of some kind on our part.

I believe it's that way with the tithe. It is an act of obedience. He says, "...for now I know..." We've said, "Well the Lord knows my heart, He knows that if I had $20 million I would tithe." If you won't tithe on $2.00, why would you do it on $20 million?

Tithing on an Inheritance

Let me say something about inheritances. Some years ago, my father passed away, and he left me some inheritance money. It was about the equivalent of a union workers yearly salary. Now, ever since my wife, Theresa and I got married, we have always tithed and have given offerings above that. But when that inheritance came, I could have written a book of excuses for not paying tithe on it!

I would lay awake at night and all kinds of thoughts would come to me about why I should not pay tithe on that inheritance. A new Harley Davidson was calling my name. The spirit of mammon was speaking to me like nobody's business!

So, you know what I did? I wrote my tithe check out and added a thousand dollars because I said I was not going to let that spirit of mammon stop me! I have to tell you, I'd always thought it would be easy to give if I got a great amount of money like that, but it wasn't! But we did it anyway because I am not going to let the spirit of mammon control my life. Money will have no hold on me whatsoever. The tithe helps us with that and puts our trust in God and not in the natural.

What Do You Treasure?

Matthew 6:19-21 NKJV
Do not lay up for yourselves treasures on earth, where moth and rust destroy and where thieves break in and steal; but lay up for yourselves treasures in heaven, where neither moth nor rust destroys and where thieves do not break in and steal. For where your treasure is, there your heart will be also.

We could basically go through a person's financial statement to find out what the treasure of their heart is. Just by looking at where they spend money, we can find out whether it is sports, traveling, houses, cars, their kids, the church, ministry; you can really find out a person's heart by where their treasure (money) is.

So, I encourage you to ask yourself, "Where is my treasure?" Just look through your finances. It doesn't take a genius. Look at where your money goes, repent of the mistakes you have made, and put God first in your finances. Your heart always connects to your treasure.

Testimony

Bob and Leia

We have always given and so it just seemed like the right thing to do to continue to tithe even when circumstances beyond our control created a situation with Bob's job, where he wasn't getting a paycheck. We continued to tithe as though that money was coming in. We went for 6 months without a paycheck and never missed a house payment or any other bills. Bob began to look for other work but the market was bleak. He was in the building industry and this was during the great fall! He applied for a job with 45 other applicants. After about a month and 3 interviews, he was chosen for the job. He received a pay increase from his previous position as well.

Darrin

I am an electrician. My wife and I have tithed ever since we got born again. Shortly before Pastor Glen started this series, I lost my job due to the downturn in the economy. We had 3 small kids at home so things got a little tight but we continued to give. I applied for a job with a firm I had always wanted to work at. There was a total of 150 applicants for the job. We prayed and believed that the job was mine and I was hired!!!

CHAPTER SIX
WHAT YOUR TITHE DOES FOR YOU

The tithe opens the windows of heaven to us.

> Malachi 3:7-10 NKJV
> Yet from the days of your fathers you have gone away from My ordinances and have not kept them. Return to Me, and I will return to you," says the Lord of hosts. "But you said, 'In what way shall we return?' "Will a man rob God? Yet you have robbed Me! But you say, 'in what way have we robbed You?' In tithes and offerings. You are cursed with a curse, for you have robbed Me, even this whole nation. Bring all the tithes into the storehouse, that there may be food in My house, and try Me now in this," says the Lord of hosts, "if I will not open for you the windows of heaven and pour out for you such blessing that there will not be room enough to receive it.

A New Perspective

Windows today are made of glass, a see-through structure. In your house, especially in the winter, you might have curtains over your windows. But if you open those curtains you can see the view outside, through the glass.

However, there were no such things as glass windows in the Old Testament. A window was carved out of wood, and you could open the shutters to look out. But there was no glass in it, it was just open to the outside elements.

So, get a picture of being cooped up in the house all winter without being able to see out the window, because opening the window meant letting the cold in. That meant the only visual perspective we could have is what was inside the house. We couldn't see outside because the windows weren't open, and our view would be very limited.

The Bible says that when we tithe, He will open the windows of heaven. Suddenly the windows are open, and now we have a perspective of things that we couldn't see before! I believe this verse means that the windows of heaven are open for tithers, giving them a new perspective of things that they didn't have before.

A Personal Story

Let me give you an example from my life. In 2001, we were blessed to be living in a very nice house in a very nice neighborhood. After owning this house for about 7 years, in September or October, we started talking about how someday we were going to own some property. We wanted an acre to five acres, and someplace that we could have a big dog.

We decided the next January 1st, to start believing God that this was going to be the year to get our house on some property. We started saying it: "We're going to have a house with acreage."
Well, because we are tithers, I believe the windows of heaven were open, and I started seeing something in my spirit. I told Theresa, my wife, that I wanted a house that looked like an estate with a long, tree-lined driveway and a fountain out in front. I don't know how many times I told her that, it was just something I kept thinking and I knew I wanted that house. We didn't know

if we were going to build it or buy it, but it was going to happen. At the time, one of our friends was working on a house that had been repossessed, and he called me to tell me we might be able to get a very good deal buying that house. I knew which house he was talking about because I had driven by it before. It had a tree-lined driveway with a fountain out front and was set back from the road.

I told Theresa, "I think this is our house!" The house was around 3300 square feet with 4 bedrooms and a den, but it was a mess. After walking through it you felt like you needed a shower. The previous owners had broken the toilets upstairs and they'd leaked down through the ceiling. The construction crew said that when they pulled out the old carpets, it was the nastiest thing they had ever seen. There were hardwood floors that looked like a roller coaster with all the ups and downs because of the water damage. The owner also brought a hose into the house and sprayed the kitchen cabinets and warped them. He wired the heat pump backwards to intentionally burn it up.

But we had invested in real estate before, so that didn't bother us at all. The property had five acres and many other things that we wanted so we said, "This is our house!" I called the bank vice-president and told him I wanted to buy that house. I offered an amount quite a bit lower than the asking price and he said he couldn't do it. Finally, over several days we settled on an amount just over the price I offered. So, I bought the house over the phone!

We rented out the house we were living in and moved into the new house. I sold my Harley and built my wife a new kitchen. The property backs up to 100 acres of county property where we can ride our four- wheeler.

We started dreaming and thinking we could live here for many years. Now it is a beautiful house, and we have plans to make it a great 'grandkid house.'

About four years after we bought the house, we got a letter in the mail from someone who wanted to buy it. Shortly after someone else came knocking on our door wanting to make us an offer on the house! We also found out it had been rezoned, and people were bidding against one another to buy it. We had an offer for $2.5 million and I thought "SOLD!"

Unfortunately, that was just at the height of the housing boom, and then the economy tanked. It isn't worth $2.5 million anymore, but it is worth a substantial amount more than we originally paid for it.

Now why did I see a house with a fountain out front and a tree-lined driveway? I thought it was because that is what I wanted. I believe the Lord put that vision in me to give me a perspective that would get me right to that specific house, so that He could bless me down the road!

I would like to tell you that my greatest real estate investment was due to my research and my awesome real estate knowledge. We bought the house for $300,000, put $30,000 into it and it was appraised for $345,000 when we bought it. Now it's obviously worth a lot more than that!

But the reality is that the greatest real estate investment I ever made was because the Lord put me right in the middle of it. I believe it's because the windows of heaven were opened, and I saw a perspective of something I couldn't see before.

Open Windows of Opportunity

I look at the windows of heaven two different ways. First, as I said above, open windows can mean a new perspective – seeing things, opportunities, through the window in a new way.

The second way your blessing might come through the open windows of heaven is through opportunities -- a new job or another stream of income that God has for you. Most of the time, the way God will bless and increase people is through a job, a financial investment, or an idea.

Oral Roberts said, "Miracles are coming toward you every hour of every day of your life. They are coming toward you or they are passing by you. It's up to you not to let that miracle pass you by." You have to believe that God has pleasure in the prosperity of His servant (see Psalm 35:27) and that there are always deals coming your way. If you walk around thinking you tithe but it will never amount to anything, then according to your faith it will happen the way you believe it (see Matthew 9:29).

God is just trying to bless and take care of His people who tithe. Theresa and I have a burning desire to give to missions and to take care of and help people all across the world. If there is one thing that bothers us, it is watching our people not prosper in every realm of their lives. This is why we exist. This is why we pastor a church. It is to see people blessed financially, blessed in their marriages, blessed with healing, blessed in every area of life. I wrote this book because I am trying to get something to you and be a blessing to you!

The Tithe Must "Die"

The next part of this teaching is what I believe is a Biblical principle. I can substantiate the other facts about tithing from the Word, but there is not dogmatic biblical evidence for this point, although I believe the principle is here.

I believe that we must let our tithe or seed die. By that I mean, there must be a place where we don't have any say over our tithe; we just put it in a bucket and we don't get to designate where it goes.

> John 12:24 NKJV
> Most assuredly, I say to you, unless a grain of wheat falls into the ground and dies, it remains alone; but if it dies, it produces much grain.

I believe there has to be some giving in our life that has to fall to the ground and die. In other words, once we give it, we have no say over it in any way. We simply put it into the general fund of a local church, then we trust the pastoral staff of the church to use that money wisely for the daily operations of the church. This provides a way for them to minister to people of all ages within the church and in the community.

An offering is above our tithe, it is a specific designation, to a person, project, event, or area of the church. Some people use their offerings to seek the favor of other people but there has to be giving in our life where we just totally abandon our hearts and where we completely release it. This is the tithe. It is just something that we give to the Lord, and from that point forward it dies to us.

Release It

There was a time when Theresa and I believed God for a boat. Our son, Joel, was in high school, and we had some wonderful family times with that boat. After Joel graduated from high school, the Lord spoke to us about giving our boat away, so we did. I told the person we gave it to that there were no strings attached. I told him that if he decided to take the title of the boat, turn around and sell it tomorrow for the money, I would not be offended. Once I give something, it is dead to me. If I give you a coat, then see someone else wearing it the next week, I have no problem with that. I gave it to you – now it's yours. I released it. There are things in our lives that we are to give, and we can't get upset about how they're used after we give them. I believe the tithe is like that. When we give our tithe, it has to die in our lives. Matthew 6:6 says, "Your Father who sees in secret will Himself reward you openly." It is a heart issue.

The Tithe Brings Meat into the House of God

Malachi 3:10 NKJV
Bring all the tithes into the storehouse, that there may be food in My house, and try Me now in this," says the Lord of hosts, "if I will not open for you the windows of heaven and pour out for you such blessing that there will not be room enough to receive it.

The King James Version of the Bible uses the word 'meat' here instead of 'food' – it means something that gives us sustenance or strength; something that feeds us.

There are two ways to look at this. First, when we bring the tithe into the storehouse – the church – it puts meat, or strength, into the church. It brings sustenance to the local body. In other words, it helps to facilitate all the things that go into running a church: supplies for the everyday operations of the building, curriculum and supplies for the children and youth, printed communications and information, music, and media production -- to name a few.

It costs money to get the gospel out, whether we like it or not. Most of us want to sit on a chair when we go to church on Sunday – that costs something. Most of us want our worship team to worship – that costs money too. We want our children to be well cared for and taught well – that costs money. We want a place for our youth to come to that they are proud of and want to invite their friends. It has to be fun, exciting and energized – that costs money. We want to proudly invite our friends to church and not have to walk around holes in the carpet or walls or broken chairs – that costs money. Think of the daily operations of your home and now think of the operations of God's home. The tithe makes sure the natural needs of the local church can be met.

Second, the tithe brings spiritual meat into the house. What does that mean? When I get up in the pulpit every week, I want to have a word for my congregation that will help them change. The tithe is part of paying my salary, and the salary of the staff, so we can be available to meet the needs of the people and be a place of refuge for the hurting and hopeless. We want to be a place where you can bring your friends and family, when you may not know how to minister to them, but you know you can bring them to church and direct them to someone that can. Or you can attend a class and learn how to lead someone in a prayer of salvation. Spiritual food is better for us than physical food. When we bring our tithes to the local church, we help provide the spiritual sustenance, the revelation and spirit of truth, that people need.

> Deuteronomy 28:8 NKJV
> The Lord will command the blessing on you in your storehouses and in all to which you set your hand, and He will bless you in the land which the Lord your God is giving you.

There is a storehouse principle in the Word of God. God is a storehouse kind of God.

Have you ever noticed that God does things extravagantly?

When He built a temple, it was so full of gold, it was dazzling. When He put water on the Earth, He didn't just make a couple of lakes, He built oceans that are not just deep enough for ships but miles deep. He fed 5,000 people with just a few loaves and fish, and there were 12 baskets left over!

God is a God of abundance. He is a God of storehouses. It would do all of us good to realize that we all need a storehouse. The church needs a storehouse. You need a storehouse.

What is a storehouse? In our society today, you don't need a barn to put grain in or cattle in. You just need to open a savings account and put something in it. Some people are waiting until something happens to them to put something in their savings account, but I submit to you to start with $1, $2 or $5 a week! Soon it will add up, and the next thing you know, in 10 years, you will be putting $500 a week in there because God will start blessing your storehouse. I believe churches should have storehouses too.

The Storehouse Principle

God wants us to live in an economy that is different than the world's. When you live within the storehouse principal you are free to do things other people aren't.

I think about the story of Joel Osteen. He started out working behind the scenes doing camera work for his dad's church, Lakewood Church in Houston, Texas. His dad, Pastor John Osteen, lived on the storehouse principle. He used to say if he could believe God to get ahead for one week, then he could believe God to get ahead for two weeks. So, he would save his money and get ahead two weeks.

Then, John started saying if he could believe God for two

weeks, he could believe Him for three weeks and four weeks and five weeks. When he wanted to buy a building, he would figure out how much it would cost, make those payments into the storehouse, then buy the building with cash. I don't know the exact numbers, but when John died he probably had several years of church's income saved up in a storehouse.

So, when his son Joel took over the church, he never thought about how they were going to pay the bills. He just started preaching, and the next thing you know they bought a coliseum in Houston, did a $60 million remodel, and now he has the largest church in America. How? Because of the storehouse principle. It is important for us to realize that the church should have a storehouse, and each of us personally should have one too. It will help us in our long-term financial situations.

Testimony

Jerry

My wife and I believe strongly in giving. I got called into my boss' office. I figured I was getting laid off because the economy was so bad and business was down. I was blown away when instead I got a $9.00 an hour raise.

David

After hearing this teaching, I received a $5000.00 bonus at work. I thought it was a mistake and tried to give back or at least find out why I got it. They wouldn't take it back. They said I had earned it. A short time later I got notice that my division had done so well this year that I received a yearly bonus for $53,000! That's "Windows of Heaven opened on you" blessing!

Joe

I believe in tithing and giving offerings. While going to school I waited tables. One night I received a $330.00 tip from one person. That night I made over $400. I was short on my school tuition and was able to pay it off.

CHAPTER SEVEN
THE TITHE CREATES A PARTNERSHIP

Numbers 18:24 NKJV
For the tithes of the children of Israel, which they offer up as a heave offering to the Lord, I have given to the Levites as an inheritance; therefore I have said to them, "Among the children of Israel they shall have no inheritance."

Technically speaking, in the Old Testament the tithe went to the Levitical priesthood, who were the ministers of that day.

Let me explain. There were 12 tribes of Israel. God said He was going to give Israel the Promised Land. He split the land up evenly to 11 tribes as their inheritance, but He didn't give any land to the 12th tribe because that was the priesthood. The priests were to get the tithes from the people and that's what they lived on. In the natural, it was a partnership between the ministers of the day and the people.

Today we pay our tithe to the church and it frees up the ministers to pray and study. As a Pastor, it means that I don't have to work another job, but can spend my time thinking about my congregation and their families. It means that our church staff can spend time praying for people, preparing messages, getting people healed, getting the lost into the kingdom of God, and blessing people. It means our whole lives can revolve around the church and the work of the ministry.

When people walk into a church, they want the youth group to be amazing. They want the Pastor to feed them the Word. They want excellent worship. They don't say it with their mouth but it is said with their attendance. Everyone is looking for a church that has a great word, great worship, great youth ministry and great children's ministry.

There is only one way to get all those things, and that is to bring the tithe into the storehouse so that we can properly take care of the people who come there. The tithe belongs to the local church. It's not meant to be split up and given to many different ministries.

Now, offerings are different. Offerings are anything you give above your tithe. We can do whatever we want with our offerings. Theresa and I give our tithe to our own local church, and we give most of our offerings here too, although some goes to other places, as well. We support a girl in Thailand that was almost sold in to sex slavery when she was young and we have been supporting her every month for about 8 years. We also support a widow in the Philippines, and a few missionaries sent out from our church.

It is important to realize that the tithe is a partnership between the ministry and the people, to make sure there is food and sustenance in the house. It is absolutely essential.

Testimony

Pam

I am a real estate agent. During the recession, no one was moving inventory. People weren't buying or selling homes, but my husband and I believe we have rights as tithers. The word says He will rebuke the devourer for our sakes. During this time, I hit my Real Estate Cap and now when selling a property, I get 100% commissions!

CHAPTER EIGHT
THE TITHE REBUKES THE DEVOURER

Malachi 3:7-11 NKJV
Yet from the days of your fathers you have gone away from My ordinances and have not kept them. Return to Me, and I will return to you," says the Lord of hosts. "But you said, 'in what way shall we return?' "Will a man rob God? Yet you have robbed Me! But you say, 'in what way have we robbed You?' In tithes and offerings. You are cursed with a curse, for you have robbed Me, even this whole nation. Bring all the tithes into the storehouse, that there may be food in My house, and try Me now in this," says the Lord of hosts, "if I will not open for you the windows of heaven and pour out for you such blessing that there will not be room enough to receive it. "And I will rebuke the devourer for your sakes, so that he will not destroy the fruit of your ground, nor shall the vine fail to bear fruit for you in the field," says the Lord of hosts.

This scripture says that the devourer will be rebuked when we tithe. Here's a personal example to illustrate. My wife, Theresa, and I have dabbled in real estate and we used to have some rental houses. We had certain renters who paid on time and certain renters who didn't. We would never tell our renters that we were ministers, but somehow, they would find out and then some of them wouldn't want to pay their rent.

They would say, "Why are you demanding our rent? I thought you were Christians!" Well, on some of those rental houses the mortgage payment might be $800 and we were only getting $750 in rent. So, when the renter didn't pay us, we still had a whole mortgage that had to be paid!

I noticed that when people would get behind in their rent, they would never come to me and demand that I fix something. But those who were current on rent didn't hesitate to call me. I had one woman call me while I was in the Philippines and wanted me to come fix her garbage disposal. She demanded her rights as a renter because she paid her rent on time.

I have always looked at the tithe that same way. When my tithe is paid, then I have rights and privileges. I have those rights and privileges anyway because Jesus bought and paid for them, but in my mind, knowing I have paid my tithe helps me to stand there and tell the devil to take his hands off my stuff.

Two Guys Get a Moose

One of my dreams has always been to go on a moose hunt. My father-in-law and I planned a hunting trip to Canada. I invited my friend, Byron, to join us. We drove up there and rode into the woods on horseback to go hunting.

There were seven hunters in two different camps, and each group had a guide. Our paths never crossed with the other group, but we would radio back and forth to see if they had seen anything.

On the first day we were out on horseback all day and didn't see anything; day two, nothing, day three nothing, day four nothing. On day five, we saw a squirrel. Day six came and still no moose. The guides started saying that it wasn't a good time to hunt moose because the rut (mating season) was already over and it was too late in the year.

Well, I looked at my friend and I said, "Byron, I'm a tither and you're a tither. We paid a lot of money for this moose hunt. If God has to bring me a moose from 100 miles away, he had better get trotting right now because I am going to shoot a moose." Byron said, "That is right. I agree with you Pastor and we are going to shoot a moose."

On the seventh day, Byron and I were walking along an open field with our guide next to some trees and I thought I saw a moose. I told the guide and he said, "Yes, that is a moose!" So, we snuck around the field to the moose and the guide told me to stay by one of the trees while he and Byron went around to cut the moose off. About 30 minutes later I heard a couple of shots, and when I rushed up there, I found that Byron had gotten himself a moose!

The next day came and went, and still no moose for me. The following day I was with the same guide and we decided to go back to the same area where we shot the other moose. We were in a tree line by an open field and were walking along when the guide said, "Did you hear that? I think I heard a moose!"

We changed direction, went about 50 yards, and suddenly, I heard a moose! Over the next hour, I had one of the most amazing hunting experiences of my entire life, and I shot a moose.

Out of all seven guys on that hunting trip, the only ones who shot a moose were the two tithers. You may say that is a coincidence, and you can go ahead and believe that. But it just so happens that the two guys that claimed their tithing rights got their moose. You ask, "Can you do that?" It worked for me. I can have only what I believe God for, nothing more and nothing less.

Don't Let the Devil Steal Your Blessing

Don't let the devil rob you of your financial blessing. Prove God in this, just like He said to do. God is not out to curse you and steal from you. He is only trying to get a blessing to you. Give the tithe to the Lord and you will be blessed. It works just like He said it would. Let's honor God with our tithe.

Testimony

Marcus

I had $1800.00 for my rent in my wallet when I went to Walmart to pick up a few things. While walking into the store I dropped it and someone picked it up. I did not even realize it was missing. Another person saw the person who picked it up and ran after me. He told me who had it. I was able to run after them and get it back!!! Devourer rebuked!

PRAYER

Father God, I see in Your Word that the tithe is holy. I repent of not tithing and I decide now to tithe. It's not that I have to tithe but that I get to tithe. I thank You for pouring out a blessing on me as You said in Your Word. I also thank You for pouring out a blessing upon my church. I want to be on Your system, Father and not the world's system. I give all I am to You, including my finances and I thank You for opening the windows of heaven over my life so that I may be a greater blessing to people everywhere I go. In Jesus name, Amen.

ABOUT THE AUTHOR

Glen Johnson is the Senior Pastor at Faith Center Church founded in 1982. Currently there are two campuses, a Bible College, and Rom517 Recovery.

He holds a Master of Theology from Eastcoast Christian College. He and his wife, Theresa, serve together with their son Joel and daughter-in-law Sarah. Joel and Sarah have 3 children. Glen and Theresa love spending time with their grandchildren and traveling.

Made in the USA
Middletown, DE
12 February 2021

33525903R10038